Books in This Series

Better Baseball for Boys
Better Basketball for Boys
Better Basketball for Girls
Better Bicycling for Boys and Girls
Better BMX Riding and Racing for Boys and Girls
Better Cross-Country Running for Boys and Girls
Better Field Events for Girls
Better Field Hockey for Girls
Better Football for Boys
Better Gymnastics for Girls
Better Horseback Riding for Boys and Girls
Better Ice Skating for Boys and Girls
Better Karate for Boys
Better Kite Flying for Boys and Girls
Better Roller Skating for Boys and Girls
Better Skateboarding for Boys and Girls
Better Soccer for Boys and Girls
Better Softball for Boys and Girls
Better Swimming for Boys and Girls
Better Synchronized Swimming for Girls

Better Tennis for Boys and Girls
Better Track for Girls
Better Volleyball for Girls
Better Weight Training for Boys

BMX bikes, light in weight but very strong, have triggered a revolution in cycling.

BETTER BMX RIDING AND RACING

for Boys and Girls

George Sullivan

Illustrated with photographs and diagrams

DODD, MEAD & COMPANY · NEW YORK

Many people contributed in the preparation of this book. Special thanks are due Jim Cerullo, Braddock Moto-X Raceway, North Bergen, New Jersey; Ken Aman and Russ Okawa, BMX Products, Inc.; Rodney Keeling, American Bicycle Association; Fran Durst, National Bicycle League; Bob Haro, Haro Designs; Francesca Kurti; TLC Custom Labs; and Aime La-Montagne.

The author is also grateful to the many boys and girls who posed for the photos that appear in the book, including Keith LaPointe, Mike Chupak, John Sachel, Marc Jeffries, Dennis Bodtman, and Billy Sargent.

PICTURE CREDITS

BMX Products, Inc., 8, 19 (right); Neil Katine, 13, 52 (bottom), 53; Aime LaMontagne, 14 (right), 18, 29 (left); Powerlite, 14 (left); Sugino Cycle, Inc., 17 (left; Vector BMX, USA, 12 (left). All other photographs are by George Sullivan.

3 4 5 6 7 8 9 10

Library of Congress Cataloging in Publication Data

Sullivan, George, 1927–
  Better BMX riding and racing for boys and girls.

  Summary: Introduces the sport of bicycle motocross, an indoor or outdoor bicycle-racing sport similar to cross-country motorcycle racing across rugged terrain.
    1. Bicycle motocross—Juvenile literature.
  [1. Bicycle motocross. 2. Bicycle racing] I. Title.
  II. Title: Better BMX riding and racing for boys and girls.
  GV1049.3.S84 1984   796.6   83-25440
  ISBN 0-396-08331-5
  ISBN 0-396-08376-5 (pbk.)

CONTENTS

BMX racers at a North Bergen, New Jersey, track.

RIDING AND RACING

An electronic horn blares. The starting light flashes green. Helmeted riders on small, knobby-tired bikes explode out of the starting gate. Dirt flies.

There are screams of "Go, Jeff, go!" and "Come on, Mike, you can do it!"

The riders rip down a gentle slope leading to a steeply banked turn, a "berm" to BMXers. Out of the turn, they streak toward a series of bone-rattling "whoops"—or bumps. The main feature of the course is a "tabletop," a flat-topped jump that sends bikes soaring.

Despite the obstacles, speeds exceed 30 miles an hour. Each race lasts about 50 seconds.

This is BMX racing, recognized as the most popular children's sports activity since Little League baseball was founded in 1939.

BMX is an abbreviation for bicycle motocross. The name comes from conventional motocross in which adult competitors race lightweight motorcycles over rugged courses. (The term motocross itself is a blend of "motorcycle" and "cross-

Steeply banked turns are called berms.

Ken Aman, 17, of Highland, New York, has been racing and winning for four years.

country.") A motocross race is also called a scramble, a good name.

BMX racing with sturdy, pared-down bicycles dates to the late 1960s and early 1970s when boys and girls in California began to mimic motorcycle daredevils by racing their bikes on hills and vacant lots where they lived.

The sport developed slowly at first. During the late 1970s, it began to take off. It got a big boost in 1982 with the release of the movie *E.T., The Extra-Terrestrial*. The young actors in the film were shown riding BMX bikes.

Today, according to the Bicycle Manufacturers Association of America, about 40 percent of all bicycles sold in the United States are BMX bikes. An estimated three million boys and girls own them.

There are more than 700 BMX tracks in operation throughout the country, ranging from 600 to 1,400 feet in length. Most are outdoor courses, but some are well-constructed enclosed structures. A single track offers as many as 50 or 60 races on the average day.

Tens of thousands of boys and girls compete regularly in the hundreds of national and local BMX races. These are divided by age, sex, and degree of skill—beginner, novice, expert, and pro. Age classifications range from 6-and-under to 17-and-over. Prizes usually take the form of trophies and bike shop gift certificates.

To some BMX competitors and their parents, the

California's Cassandra Adams, a leading BMX rider.

Riders compete for trophies and bike shop gift certificates.

9

Wheelies are a mainstay of freestyle riding.

sport is much more than a simple leisure-time activity; it's a mania. Weekends are spent on the road looking for new tracks on which to compete. Vacations are also devoted to the sport. Some families purchase big motor homes to shuttle young riders from one course to another. Families can spend many thousands of dollars on BMX equipment each year. (A BMX bike costs from $200 to over $1,000.)

"It's a family thing," says Jimmy Cerullo, owner of the Braddock Moto-X Raceway in North Bergen, New Jersey. "The whole family turns out once a week, and they have a good time together. How many other activities can do that?"

How can you find out about BMX racing in your area? Check at a local bike shop, one that specializes in BMX equipment. Inquire where the local tracks are.

Or you can write one or both of the two national organizations that sanction BMX racing—the American Bicycle Association and the National Bicycle League. Their addresses are listed in the final chapter of this book. Request a list of tracks in your area. You might also want to ask for a beginning rider's information packet.

Of course, not all BMX riding involves competition. Hundreds of thousands of youngsters ride BMX bikes just for fun, bouncing over curbs or performing "wheelies," that is, riding on the rear wheel alone by pulling up on the front of the bike.

Just goofing around has led to another branch of the sport—freestyle BMX, or trick riding. Freestyling enthusiasts often build ramps in their backyards that enable them to indulge in rollbacks, kickturns, aerials, and many other such maneuvers.

Maybe you're interested in owning a BMX bike so you can compete at a track near your home. Maybe you want to freestyle on local streets. Either way, you're due for plenty of fun and excitement.

CHOOSING A BIKE

BMX bikes are available in a wide range of styles. They also vary in weight and strength, two highly critical factors.

Visit a bike shop, and you may find yourself involved in a long discussion concerning the merits of different kinds of bike frames, forks, handlebars, wheels, tires, and other components. Indeed, shopping for a BMX bike can be a bewildering experience—unless you know exactly what you want. This chapter is meant to help you make up your mind.

BMX bikes are 20-inch bikes. That means they ride along on wheels that are 20 inches in diameter. (The wheel is measured from the outside surface of the tire, not from rim edge to rim edge.) However, very young riders, those, say, six or seven years old or younger, usually own bikes with 16-inch wheels.

Adult riders—and there are some—pedal along on bikes with 24- or 26-inch wheels. Such machines compete in what is called the cruiser class.

BMX bikes are made of tough, lightweight metals. Tempered chrome-molybdenum, called chrome-moly, is highly favored for frames, forks, handlebars, stems, and other parts.

The first decision you have to make in buying a BMX bike is whether you're going to purchase a stock bike or assemble a machine from components

bought individually. A stock bike is a fully assembled bike, purchased right off the shelf, so to speak.

At one time, the selection of stock bikes was somewhat limited. But not any more. Today, there are several different companies that offer stock bikes that boast quality parts and workmanship. Such bikes cost from $250 to $350.

Purchase your bike in a shop that specializes in BMX machines. Ask the owner or a salesperson to explain all of the differences between an inexpensive bike and an expensive one. You will learn a great deal from the explanation.

Many riders prefer to assemble their own bikes from components. This assures that the buyer will get exactly what he or she wants in the way of a frame, handlebars, wheels, and so forth. A bike that is assembled piece-by-piece can cost twice as much as a stock bike, however.

The pages that follow discuss the most important bike parts. The information they contain is intended to be helpful to you whether you're buying a stock bike or purchasing parts and assembling the bike yourself.

FRAME—The frame is the bike's most important supporting member. It is to your bike what a foundation is to a house.

The frame is made of metal tubing welded together to form three triangles. There is one front

11

BMX frame (pictured here with fork) is light in weight but very strong.

triangle and two rear triangles. The front and rear triangles are joined by a common base, which is the vertical tube that serves as the seat support. It is called the seat tube.

Most bike frames are made of metal tubing that is welded together at the seams. In welding, the ends of the two pieces to be joined are melted, and the molten metal flows together to create the joint. A welding "rod" is melted at the same time to fill in any spaces that might occur.

The weakest parts of the frame are usually where the metal tubes are welded together. Cracks sometimes occur close to the weld where the metal was weakened by the heat of the welding torch.

Bicycle tubing can also be joined by brazing. In this process, a brazing metal acts like glue to hold the two tubes together. Since the brazing metal melts at a lower temperature than the tube metal, the process does not require as much heat. The weakening and cracking common to welding is less likely to occur.

Sometimes metal braces, called gussets, are added at the point where one piece of tubing meets another. These strengthen the joints.

Other times frames are double-butted. This means that the metal tubes are thicker at the ends. Double-butting makes for a stronger frame but also a heavier one.

Pay close attention, not only to how the frame is constructed, but also to how much it weighs. Top-flight riders specify frames that weigh about three or four pounds.

Brazing, evidenced by metal "glue" at joints, gives added strength.

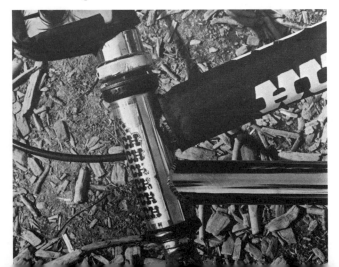

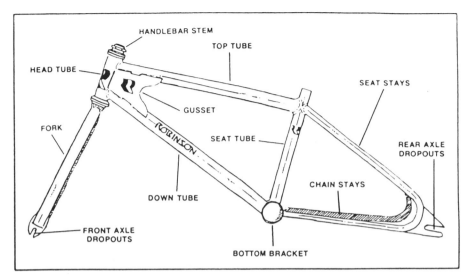

Diagram labels: HANDLEBAR STEM, TOP TUBE, HEAD TUBE, SEAT STAYS, GUSSET, FORK, SEAT TUBE, REAR AXLE DROPOUTS, CHAIN STAYS, DOWN TUBE, FRONT AXLE DROPOUTS, BOTTOM BRACKET, ROBINSON

FRONT FORK—The front fork is the steering assembly that holds the front wheel. It consists of a rod that divides into two legs. The front wheel fits between two dropouts—slots—at the fork ends.

As in the case of the frame, you want a fork that is both strong and light. If possible, buy one that weighs about 1½ pounds. The fork should be made by the same company that manufactured the frame.

The fork, when fixed to the frame, has to be properly slanted. Otherwise, the bike won't steer properly. If the fork is slanted too far forward, you lose the ability to turn sharply. If the fork is too close to being vertical, you risk spinning out when you attempt to turn.

HANDLEBARS—The entire bike is controlled through the handlebars, so it is important to get bars of the right style and shape. The width of the bars—the distance from handle to handle—is very important. The width can vary from 24 inches to 28 inches.

Anytime you pull up on the handlebars and crank down on the pedals, seeking to generate the utmost power, the bars play a crucial role. If they should be either too narrow or too wide for you, you will lose power when you pull. Experiment with bars of different widths until you find a set that feels right.

The bars, which are usually made of an aluminum alloy, or chrome-moly, and are reinforced with a straight or V-shaped cross brace, clamp firmly into

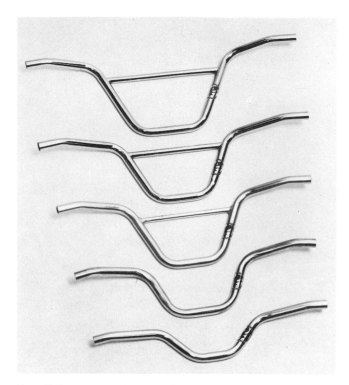

Handlebars come in a wide range of sizes and styles.

the stem, or gooseneck. The stem, in turn, fits into the headset tube, which is mounted atop the front fork. Since even the slightest slippage can be disasterous during a race, four bolts are often used to lock the bars in place.

Keep the handlebars relatively low so you don't have to reach for them. Yet they shouldn't be so

14

Sturdy mag wheels are virtually indestructible.

low that your knees strike the bars as you pedal. Grips of soft rubber or composition material attach to the bar ends.

SADDLE—Pick out a racing saddle, a saddle that is unpadded. A padded saddle adds extra weight.

Most riders adjust the saddle so that it is relatively low. In a race, when you are standing and pedaling, you want the saddle out of the way.

WHEELS—As mentioned earlier, BMX racing wheels are 20 inches in diameter. Wheel rims can be made of steel or an aluminum alloy. There are also mag wheels, usually made of a tough thermoplastic and brightly colored. Mag wheels can also be made of aluminum.

Mag wheels are reinforced with thick struts; they're spokeless. They're practically indestructible. For this reason, mag wheels are recommended for street riding.

In the conventional wheel, there's a hub in the center to which the spokes attach. The hub also holds the wheel bearings.

The wheel is usually fitted with number 80 spokes. This means the spoke wire is .080 inches in diameter.

TIRES—The BMX bike rides on "knobbies," tires with deep treads that dig into the dirt and send you flying along.

Tires are measured in cross-section. Most riders prefer a 1.75 rear tire, while a 2.125 tire is the most popular size for the front tire. Some riders choose a

BMX tires, with deep treads, are called knobbies.

15

1.75 tire for the front because it's lighter. But you get less traction with the smaller size.

What your bike does—any bike, not only just a BMX machine—is convert the vertical power you generate when you pedal into the horizontal power that moves the vehicle forward. What actually accomplishes this is the drive train. The various parts of the drive train are the pedals, crank, chainwheel (also called the front sprocket), and the rear sprocket (also called the cog or freewheel).

The chainwheel drives the chain that turns the rear sprocket. The rear sprocket propels the rear wheel forward.

PEDALS—BMX pedals come in a variety of shapes and styles. The best ones are made of aluminum and have hardened-steel or chrome-moly axles.

BMX racers do not use toe clips. During a race, there are times when you have to be able to move one foot or the other off a pedal and quickly thrust it to the ground in order to help maintain your balance or avoid a collision. A toe clip would hinder you.

CRANKS—The rotating cranks to which the pedals attach are somewhat longer on BMX bikes than on conventional machines. They are usually available in three sizes: 170, 175, and 180 millimeters (approximately 6½, 6¾, and 7 inches).

The longer the crank, the more power you get

BMX pedals are made of aluminum and have hardened-steel axles.

Chainwheel and 175 mm forged crank.

side-pull calipers. Both work well, but the side-pull style is preferred by most riders because it is easier to adjust.

Some bikes are equipped with both front and rear brakes. With brakes on both wheels, you can stop or slow down with greater efficiency, and thus you have greater control over your bike. But most serious riders feel that the added weight of the second set of brakes isn't worth the slight benefit that's gained.

when you pedal. A shorter crank enables you to pedal faster. As a beginner, choose an in-between size, that is, a crank of about 175 millimeters (6¾ inches).

Cranks have to be ruggedly built to withstand the abuse they take when spills or collisions occur. Specify a one-piece, forged, heat-treated crank.

BRAKES—About 95 percent of all BMX bikes are equipped with caliper brakes at the rear wheel. These are hand-operated brakes that exert pressure on both sides of the rear rim through a cable pull.

You may have to choose between center-pull and

Virtually all BMX racing bikes are equipped with rear caliper brakes.

17

Handlebar crossbar, top tube, and stem must be encased in safety padding.

You'll see BMX bikes with coaster brakes, too. These are foot-operated brakes that are housed in the hub of the rear wheel.

Coaster brakes are fine if you intend to use your bike chiefly for street riding. But in racing, coaster brakes fall short. To stop or slow down, you have to back pedal about a half a stroke. Then, to get yourself going again, you have to pedal forward, first making up the half-stroke reverse rotation before the gears take hold. This takes a second or two of valuable time. As you know, races are often won or lost in terms of parts of a second.

SAFETY PADS—The rules of BMX racing state that several bike parts, potentially dangerous in case of spills, must be padded. These parts are the handlebar crossbar, the top tube (the long, horizontal length of tubing that extends from the steering head to the seat tube), and the stem (the clamp that holds the handlebars in place). You can use strips of foam rubber and tape to do the padding. Or you can buy the special pads that several companies sell that fit these parts.

BIKE LOCKS—Always lock your bike whenever you leave it unattended, even if it's only for a minute or so. Use a case-hardened length of chain and a sturdy lock. The heavier the chain, the better. Pass the chain through the frame and rear wheel and around a stationary object, such as a pole embedded in concrete.

Kryptonite locks offer the utmost in security. A Kryptonite lock takes the form of a U-shaped, hinged shackle that is fitted with a tubular-key locking mechanism. Thieves armed with bolt cutters,

Look here for your bike's serial number.

hacksaws, pry bars, and other such tools cannot open a Kryptonite lock.

Kryptonite's Megalock/BMX is designed especially for BMX bikes. It is vinyl-covered to protect the bike's finish.

In helping to safeguard your bike, it is a good idea to record its serial number. This is found stamped into the bottom bracket of the frame. In some communities, the serial number can be registered with the police, and thus serve to identify the bike should it be stolen and then recovered.

A final word concerning equipment: Your BMX bike was designed and built for racing and, thus, it is not equipped for night riding. If it becomes necessary for you to ride at dusk or when it is dark, be sure to have the bike fitted out with a headlight, taillight, and reflectors. And be sure to wear light-colored clothing whenever you take the bike out at night.

Kryptonite's Megalock/BMX is designed especially for BMX bikes.

19

GEAR RATIOS

If you intend to become serious about racing, the matter of gear ratios becomes important. Gear ratio is the numerical expression of the relationship between the front sprocket (or chainwheel) and the rear sprocket.

To find a bike's gear ratio, you divide the number of teeth in the front sprocket by the number of teeth in the rear sprocket. Here's an example, a bike with 40 teeth in the front sprocket and 20 teeth in the rear sprocket.

$$\frac{40 \text{ (teeth in front sprocket)}}{20 \text{ (teeth in rear sprocket)}} = 2.00 \text{ (gear ratio)}$$

A gear ratio of 2.00 means that everytime you pump the front sprocket around a full revolution, you rotate the rear sprocket (and rear wheel) two times.

Standard BMX bikes have 44 teeth in the front sprocket and 16 teeth in the rear sprocket, a relationship that is expressed as $44/16$. This combination gives a gear ratio of 2.75 (44 divided by 16). Everytime you turn the front sprocket one full revolution, you spin the rear wheel 2¾ times.

What is important to realize is that the higher the gear ratio, the harder it is to accelerate. But it's easier to go faster once you've gotten started.

The lower the gear ratio, the easier it is to explode away at the start. But it's more difficult to maintain top speed for a long period, since you have to churn your legs faster.

Beginning riders sometimes make the mistake of choosing a gear ratio that's higher than normal. They believe it will enable them to go faster. It does—but only after they've begun moving at a good clip.

Some bikes have easy-to-change gear systems. Owners of such machines acquire extra front and rear sprockets of assorted sizes. Before a race, they install the gears that are best suited for the track conditions they're going to face.

On a softer-than-normal track, a smaller front sprocket and larger rear sprocket are used. This combination drives the bike through loose dirt with greater efficiency. It also helps you to get out of the starting gate fast.

For a hard track, a larger front sprocket and smaller rear sprocket are the choice. This combination makes for the greatest possible speed under ideal track conditions.

The overall trend in recent years has been toward lower-than-normal gear ratios. One popular one is $43/16$, or 2.69.

But to a great extent, the gear ratio you decide upon is a matter of personal preference. Do you want to get away fast at the start and pedal wildly

20

the rest of the way? Or would you rather be a speedster once you've left the starting gate behind? It's up to you to decide.

Some riders change gear systems at trackside to cope with different conditions they encounter.

Spills are not uncommon in BMX races.

WHAT TO WEAR

Helmets slam when riders go down. There's the clanking sound of metal striking metal. Spectators moan.

Spills and collisions occur frequently in BMX racing. Nevertheless, officials maintain that the sport is safer than football or soccer. The rugged helmets and padded uniforms that riders wear help ward off serious injury.

Here's a rundown of what you should be wearing, whether you specialize in race riding or street riding:

HELMETS—A helmet is a must, as important as having air in your tires. Even if you only use your bike for running errands or for transporting you to and from school, always wear protective headgear. This is particularly true if you ride where there is automobile traffic. Helmets are required in all BMX races, of course.

Helmets are made of lightweight but tough fiber glass. They are lined on the inside with foam rubber or other cushioning materials.

There are two basic types of helmets. The best type is called the full-face helmet. It not only protects your head and ears, but also the sides of your face and your chin. In other words, there is an opening only for your eyes and nose.

Some riders complain that the full-face helmet is too heavy. But if the helmet fits properly, you're less likely to notice the heaviness, which is well worth the protection you get.

The other type of helmet protects only the head

Full-face helmets offer the best protection.

and ears. A chin strap holds it in place.

Helmets are built to be worn with mouthpieces or masks that protect both the mouth and nose. These attach by straps to the helmet sides. Mouthpieces must be worn in races.

Helmet visors are available to keep the sun out of your eyes.

Long-sleeved shirts protect the arms.

Elbow pads are required in race competition.

Expect to pay from $50 to $100 for a BMX helmet. They come in a wide range of sizes. Be sure to take the time to get a proper fit.

SHIRTS—A long-sleeved shirt or blouse should be worn to protect your arms from scratches and bruises. If you're a BMX competitor, you'll no doubt want to wear a colorful jersey blazoned with the name of your team and sponsor instead of a conventional shirt or blouse.

Wear elbow pads for added protection. Some jerseys have built-in pads at the elbows. Elbow pads are mandatory in race competition.

PANTS—The pants you wear can be of any heavy material. Tight-legged denim jeans are fine.

Remember, there is no chain guard on a BMX bike, so the right pant leg below the knee must be wrapped, tied, or clipped, so it won't get tangled between the chain and chainwheel.

Special BMX pants, called leathers, are made of heavy-duty nylon or other synthetic material, and offer padded knees, hip pads, and shin guards. Like BMX jerseys, they are available in a wide array of bright colors.

FOOTWEAR—Several manufacturers now offer special shoes for BMX riding. They have soles of soft rubber or synthetic material that help the shoes cling to the pedals. They come in both high-top and low-cut styles. High-tops are recommended because they protect the ankle from scratches and scrapes.

GLOVES—Gloves are often worn in racing com-

Pants, called leathers, are padded at the knees.

BMX shoes, like these Vans, are available in both high- and low-top styles.

There is a slip-on style, too.

petition, although they're not required. They're padded to protect the back of the hand.

Dressing up like a BMX professional can be costly. But it's also possible to enjoy the sport wearing a pair of jeans, any long-sleeved shirt, running shoes or sneakers—plus a helmet. There's really no necessity to make a big investment in clothing and accessories.

BMX gloves protect the back of the hand.

BASIC TECHNIQUES

Before you think about entering your first race, work to become a skilled rider. Racing, even in the beginner and novice classes, is not for the inexperienced.

Find a park or open lot where you can practice on soft dirt. Begin by getting used to the bike and the way in which it handles.

Pedal easily at first. Be sure each foot is positioned so the ball of the foot is resting on the pedal. This enables you to generate the most power.

If you learned to ride on a bike with coaster brakes and later owned one, you may find the BMX machine a little bit tricky. It is likely to take you some time to get accustomed to squeezing the levers mounted on the handlebars to stop the bicycle.

"I was used to coaster bikes when I first tried a BMX bike," champion rider Ken Aman recalls, "and I had a terrible time. I couldn't remember to use the hand brakes. I was even dragging my feet to try to get the bike to stop."

When it comes to steering and control, the BMX bike responds faster than a conventional two-wheeler. It also takes some time to get used to this feature. This is another reason you shouldn't try anything fancy at first.

Once you feel comfortable in riding and con-

Practice in a park or open lot.

Position the ball of your foot on the pedal.

trolling the bike, try some more advanced skills. Try making turns without slowing down. The first few times, don't go too fast. Then gradually increase your speed.

Try to keep pedaling as you make the turn. If you do need to slow down, just touch the brakes. That's what expert riders do.

When practicing a turn, should you lean over so far that you start losing your balance, simply put your inside foot to the ground. This stops you from going down—a wipeout.

If you're a natural right-hander, you'll probably

Keep pedaling throughout the turn.

On banked turns, use your inside foot to keep you balanced—if you have to.

feel more comfortable making turns to the left, and they will be easier for you. If this is true, devote most of your practice time to right turns.

When you feel confident about turning to the right or left at good speeds on the flat, try some banked turns. Perhaps there is a track near your home where you can practice.

Again, try to pedal all the way through the turn. Keep the bike positioned so its wheels are perpendicular to the track at all times. If the bike should start leaning too far to the inside, put your inside foot to the ground to prevent a spill.

Suppose you want to coast while going through a banked turn. Remember to push hard with your outside foot on the outside pedal. This gets the outside pedal in a down position. The inside pedal goes up—high above the ground. It's thus less likely to nick the ground as you bank, and trigger a spill.

Besides turns, practice stops. While traveling at a good rate of speed, apply your brakes and bring the bikc to a controlled stop.

Once you've mastered these basic skills, your next step is to try some freestyle maneuvers. A few are described in the chapter that follows.

FREESTYLE

Flashy freestyle riding may look easy but it requires plenty of practice. Don't expect to be able to perform the tricks described and pictured in this chapter without repeating them over and over.

Take it easy at first. Be patient.

One other piece of advice before you begin: To become a freestyle expert, a rider who is able to draw oohs and aahs from spectators, you need a bike that's equipped, not with caliper brakes, but with coaster brakes. Coaster brakes are those you activate with your feet by applying back pressure on the pedals. The moves described in this chapter, however, can be performed with either coaster brakes or the caliper type.

WHEELIE—The wheelie is as basic to BMX riding as swinging a bat is to baseball. Once you learn to ride with the front wheel off the ground, you can go on to perform a wide range of other tricks.

It's not difficult to do a wheelie with a BMX bike. This is because the BMX machine is much lighter in the front than in the back.

As you pedal at medium speed, simply shift your body weight to the rear and pull up on the handlebars. This gets the front wheel off the ground. Hold the wheel up for a second or two, then let it slip gently back to the ground.

Keep repeating this drill, increasing the height of

To do a wheelie, simply shift your body weight back and pull up on the handlebars.

31

For a curb endo, spring upward off the seat as the front wheels touch the curb, and push forward on the handlebars.

the wheel and the amount of time it is in the air. Just get the feel of things.

You will eventually be able to hold the wheel at the point of balance as you continue to pedal. When the wheel starts to go down, pull up. When the wheel gets too high and you feel as if you might be going to flip over, push down.

With practice, you'll get so you can pedal relatively long distances with the front wheel in the air. Indeed, your bike will come to resemble a unicycle.

CURB ENDO—An endo is something like a reverse wheelie. It's a trick in which the rear wheel comes off the ground instead of the front wheel. The term endo comes from "end-over-end," which is the way in which you'll go flying if you don't control your speed when performing endo-related stunts.

You can perform an endo against almost any stationary object—a concrete parking lot divider or, as shown here, a curbstone.

Approach the curb at low speed, seated, and with both feet on the pedals. As the front wheel touches the curb, spring upward off the seat and push forward on the handlebars.

As the rear wheel comes off the ground, bend your knees and continue pushing. Keep the rear wheel in the air for as long as you can.

Eventually, gravity will take its course. As the rear wheel touches down, flex your knees and use your arms to cushion the impact.

FLYING—"Taking air" is the term riders use to describe what happens when you go over a high jump. There's nothing more exciting. But begin with mere mounds before you tackle high jumps.

Pedal like mad as you approach the jump. A few feet before you reach it, start coasting. Keep your pedals level.

Then lift yourself off the saddle and pull up on the front end of the bike—just as if you were doing a wheelie.

Try low jumps before tackling high ones.

In performing a kickturn on a ramp, shift your weight to the rear and pull up on the handlebars—

Now you're flying, both wheels off the ground. Shift your weight to the rear and pull up on the bars so the rear wheel becomes lower than the front wheel. You want the rear wheel to touch down first, a split second before the front wheel.

The instant that the rear wheel makes contact, shift your weight forward. Push down on the bars to get the front wheel down. Be sure to keep the front wheel pointed straight ahead. If it is turned in one direction or the other, it could brake your forward momentum and result in a nasty spill.

RAMP RIDING—Once you become skilled at trick riding on flat land, the next step is to become a ramp rider. Many young bikers build their own backyard ramps, similar to the one pictured here. Ramp riding offers countless opportunities for new

34

as when doing a wheelie; then pivot around on the rear wheel.

tricks. You can do ramp endos and wheelies, plus rollbacks, spins, jumps, and a variety of kickturns.

In performing the basic kickturn, pedal toward the ramp at medium speed. As you hit the ramp, you should be standing with the pedals level.

Shift your weight to the rear and pull up on the handlebars—as if you are doing a wheelie. As the front wheel comes up, apply the brakes. Then pivot around on the rear wheel until you are facing in the opposite direction. Lower the front wheel and pedal down the ramp.

There are many other tricks you can do, with or without a ramp. But proceed slowly. Never attempt any trick that you feel might be beyond your capabilities. You could damage your bicycle. You could also damage your body.

ALL ABOUT TRACKS

No two BMX tracks are exactly alike. But all have similar characteristics that are meant to test riders' skills.

Tracks are anywhere from 600 to 1,400 feet in length. The twisting, turning route each track takes is usually bordered with bales of hay or discarded automobile tires.

Adjacent to the track itself are the pit and holding areas. The last named is a section set aside for storing bicycles before a race. Riders and mechanics perform repairs and tune-ups within the holding area. It's also where race officials inspect the bikes.

The pit area, where last-minute preparations are made, is located close to the starting line. Usually there is one for each class. Only race riders are permitted within the pit area.

To assure a fast getaway, the race starts at the crest of a gentle slope. The starting line stretches for about thirty feet, which is wide enough to accommodate eight bikers, although at some tracks only six riders compete at one time.

Most races are started by means of an electronic starting gate. The gate consists of a long, hinged plank that sits atop the starting line. Tilted on edge, it serves as a low fence, blocking the front wheels

Fans urge on riders at Braddock Moto-X Raceway in North Bergen, New Jersey.

At race's start, hinged plank flips forward, and riders surge ahead.

Flashing light signals start.

of the bikes. At the start, the plank drops flush to the ground and the bikes are released.

Sometimes the plank is operated by a starter who calls out: "Riders get ready," "Pedals set," and "Go!" At the same instant he cries out "Go!" the starter throws a lever that drops the plank.

Other times, the movement of the plank is synchronized with a set of four starting lights that are arranged vertically, like traffic lights at an intersection. The top light is red, the two middle lights are yellow, and the bottom light is green. At the same time the bottom light flashes green, the plank drops, and the bikers explode away.

Below the starting ramp, there is usually a short stretch of level track that enables the riders to build up speed. But then they must slow down for the first turn, which can be either flat or banked. If it is banked, there is less need to slow down.

The standard turn is banked to the inside, which helps to offset the pull of centrifugal force that whizzing bicycles generate. But once in a while you may encounter an off-camber turn, one that is banked slightly to the outside. This type of turn requires less speed and a delicate touch. Otherwise, you'll find yourself among the hay bales.

Beyond a turn, there is usually another straight-away, which allows you to turn on the speed again. But watch out! Straights are frequently interrupted by jumps of one type or another. The most challenging jump is the tabletop. A ramp leads the way

Standard berm is banked to the inside, like this one.   **Tabletop jump offers riders the chance to fly high.**

up to a broad, flat surface that drops off sharply at the far edge.

Then there are whoop-de-doos, or, simply, whoops. These consist of a series of low, closely spaced jumps that can jar and jolt you almost as severely as a road pocked with potholes.

Some track layouts include short stretches of sand. You may also be confronted by a water jump. Mud pits used to be seen, but they're out of favor now. The mud not only made a mess of riders' clothes, but it clogged chains, bearings, and other moving parts.

Most tracks offer a final straight that leads to the finish line. This requires riders to pedal their hard-

Ripple in track's surface is called a whoop-de-doo.

Riders hurry along a straight leading to finish.

est in the race's final seconds.

Much of what's said above applies to outdoor tracks. In many snowbelt states, BMX racing shifts indoors during the winter months. Indoor tracks are constructed of wood or concrete. This means a different type of tire has to be used. The tread is flatter.

There are fewer jumps and other obstacles indoors, but speeds are generally faster. And there's more of an emphasis on quickness.

You've got to be more careful indoors than outdoors. Taking a spill and landing on wood or concrete is obviously more of a hazard than coming down on soft dirt.

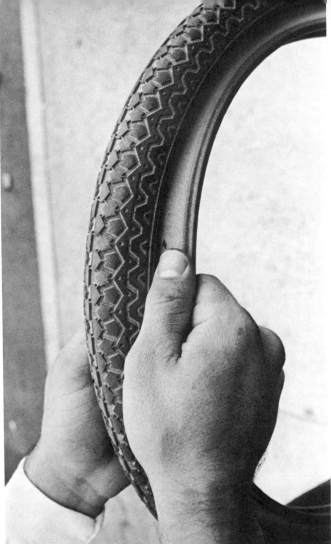

Tires for indoor racing have a flatter tread.

41

RACE PREPARATION

When you arrive at the track on the day of the race, the first thing to do is register and pay your entry fee. After you have signed up, use the free time to prepare for your first race, or moto.

First, walk over the track and plan your ride.

What line should you try to take around corners? How high should you try to go on the berms? Your walking tour of the course will help to answer such questions.

Then take a couple of practice spins around the track. Where are the loose spots? Where can you turn on the speed? Remember, in a practice run

Spend most of your time working on the start and first turn.

you don't have to hold back, fearing a fall that will cost you a good finish. You can push your luck in evaluating how far you can go on the various turns and jumps. A spill is merely going to be discomforting.

Devote a good part of your practice time to the start and the first turn. Get to know the timing of the starting gate and the cadence of the starter's call. Once you feel confident about the start and the first turn, you can begin working on the trouble spots.

You can also learn a great deal by watching skilled riders. Notice how they take the turns. Watch how high they go into the air on jumps.

You may want to make an adjustment in your tire pressure before the race, depending on the condition of the track surface. If the track is softer than usual, it might be wise to increase the tire pressure, perhaps to 45 or 50 psi (pounds per square inch). Hard tires go through sand and loose mush easier than soft tires.

If the track is hard-packed, you will probably want to reduce the air pressure to, say, 35 or 40 psi. The rubber will then grip the track surface better.

Once everyone has signed up, the moto sheets are posted. These tell you the number of the moto in which you are to compete and also give you your post position for each running of the moto. (It's standard practice to hold each moto three times.)

Moto sheets tell you when you're going to race and give you your post position.

For instance, 17—2, 7, 3 means that you are going to be competing in moto No. 17, and your gate positions are 2 in the first moto, 7 in the second moto, and 3 in the third.

Some riders, not trusting their memories, use a ballpoint pen to write their moto number and three gate positions on the back of one hand.

Sometimes only the moto numbers are given on the moto sheets. Gate numbers are assigned by a drawing that is held just before the contestants enter the starting gate.

Using the track loudspeaker, a race official an-

Bikes have to pass an official inspection.

nounces when each moto is to be run. Pay attention to these announcements. If you miss a moto, you're placed last.

Before the race, your bike will have to pass an inspection by an official who represents the organization that is sanctioning the meet. These are some of the points the inspection is likely to cover.

• Bicycle wheels can be no more than 20 inches in size, except in the case of cruiser-class bikes. These have wheels that are either 24 or 26 inches in diameter.

• The bike must have a number plate that bears your assigned number. The plate and number must be free of all decals and stickers.

• Standard motocross handlebars must be used. No unwelded extensions of the bars are permitted.

Handlebars must be fitted with hand grips.

• The handlebar crossbar, top tube, and the stem must be padded.

• The handlebars, frame, and crank cannot be cracked, damaged, or loose. Seats must be firmly attached.

• Brakes must be in good working order.

• Side stands and chain guards must be removed.

• Tires cannot be dangerously worn; they must have deep treads.

• Any axle that protrudes more than ¼ inch beyond the axle nuts must be covered with tape.

BMX has a reputation for being a safe sport. Race officials strive to uphold that reputation. Thus, if your bike fails to pass the safety inspection, you could be prohibited from taking part in the meet.

Riders are poised, feet on pedals, as they wait for the plank to fall.

46

THE START

The start is a critical part of every race. A good start enables you to pull off a holeshot, that is, tear into an early lead. Since the room for passing is so limited and the race is over so fast, you seldom have the chance to make up for a poor start.

When you hear your moto called, you and the seven riders you're competing against push your bikes up the short ramp leading to the starting gate. You will each have been assigned your own slot by this time.

"Riders ready, pedals set," the starter calls.

Straddling the seat, ease the bike into position. Then adjust the pedals, making the right pedal the high pedal, the one you're going to drive with when the gate falls.

You should have already familiarized yourself with the timing of the starting lights. "You have to know *exactly* when the gate is going to drop," says one veteran rider. "You can't guess. You have to be able to burst out of there, having your front tire about a half an inch from the gate as it is falling. Timing is the whole thing.

"Watch the lights before a race. Memorize how they're timed. At the start, when the first light flashes, look down at the gate and begin your own countdown. If you have memorized how the lights are timed, you'll know precisely when the gate is going to fall and be able to rip away."

"Wheels against the gate," says the starter.

You should be balanced on your pedals now, your hips back over the seat. Your front wheel is putting pressure on the starting plank. The final countdown is about to begin.

Tilt your head and shoulders forward over the handlebars. Keep your elbows slightly bent. Breathing deeply will help you to relax.

"Go!"

Throw your hips toward the bars as the gate starts to fall. Drive that first pedal down hard.

As the first pedal stroke ends and the second begins, shift your upper body back and begin your normal pedaling rhythm.

The first pedal gives the initial drive. The second pedal sustains that drive. Some riders say that the second pedal is even more important than the first, since the first is only half a revolution and the second is a full revolution. The third, fourth, and fifth revolutions are what propel you into a holeshot.

Most riders keep their bikes perfectly straight at the start. But some topflight riders slant their bikes a little to the left in the gate. The first powerful surge with the right foot tends to pull the bike to the right. Cocking the bike to the left compensates for that first outburst of power, and a straight start is the result. Experiment with this starting method before you try it in a race.

There are eight slots across the track. Which

As the gate starts to fall, thrust your hips forward. At the same time, drive the first pedal down hard.

one is the best? It depends. If the track turns left within a short distance of the starting gate, the No. 1 position will probably give you the greatest advantage. You'll be able to keep to the inside and thus cut down the amount of distance you have to travel around the turn. You can try to block riders who are trailing you as you negotiate the turn.

But if the track turns to the right within a short distance of the start, and you're in the No. 1 slot, you'll have to pass several riders to get to the front. With a right turn coming up, the No. 8 slot is preferred.

one). All you should think about is thrusting your weight forward at precisely the right moment, driving the right pedal down hard, and then getting the second pedal around.

Many riders tinker with their bikes in an effort to assure fast starts. They set their pedals lower or install wider bars or shorter cranks.

None of these innovations is likely to do any harm. But pulling off a holeshot depends more on timing and know-how than on any mechanical feature your bike might include. And timing and know-how can be perfected through practice.

As a general rule, don't worry about the other riders when you line up. You should concentrate on getting away at precisely the right second. Wipe everything else out of your mind. You will never get a good start if you are thinking about the other riders, about catching an elbow (or throwing

Riders pedal hard to accomplish a holeshot.

Think of a BMX race as a series of short sprints.

TACTICS AND STRATEGY

A BMX race is different from a running race. You never travel at full speed for any great length of time. As soon as you hit a straightaway, it veers into a sharp corner or becomes a jump, and you have to slow down. A BMX race is a bunch of little races, a bunch of sprints.

Your goal should be to keep your rear tire driving as hard as possible for as much of the race as possible. Brake and coast only when you have to.

Never turn around and look back during a race. Concentrate on what's happening just ahead. What's going on behind isn't important.

Jumps and turns deserve special consideration. Whenever you approach a jump, keep pedaling for as long as possible. In the case of a low jump, pull up the front end of your bike as you go over it. In other words, wheelie over it. Keep the rear tire driving.

Flying high may win cheers from the spectators, but you can't accelerate when you're airborne. Of course, in the case of tabletops and some other jumps, you have no choice but to take to the air. But the basic rule you should bear in mind states: "Air for show, down for go."

If you do have to spring clear of the ground to get over a jump, keep as low as you can. Take off with the pedals even. Let the front wheel go up naturally. If the front end starts to get too high,

In the case of low jumps and whoops, pull up on the front wheel; wheelie over them.

shift your weight forward. Try to land so the rear tire touches down before the front tire.

In the case of whoop-de-doos, pedal over them or wheelie over. Don't try to jump whoops.

Turning is decision making. Should you take the shorter but slower inside line? Or should you choose the longer but usually traffic-free outside line?

It depends on several factors.

Some general advice, first. Whenever you enter a turn, delay braking for as long as possible. Every

Land so the rear tire touches down first.

When entering a turn, delay braking for as long as possible.

extra revolution you get adds to your advantage.

Never follow another rider into a turn. First of all, you can't pass a bike that is tracking the same line you are. Equally important, if the bike in front of you should have some mishap you'll have to brake, shift your upper body forward so more weight is concentrated over the front wheel. A common mistake that beginners make is to allow the front wheel to lose traction during a turn. This reduces steering control, of course. You need the utmost in control to get around a turn fast.

Let's look at the different options you have when executing a turn. Suppose you're close to the lead as you approach the turn. Try going into the turn

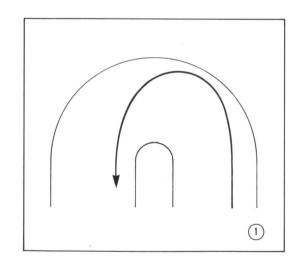

52

on the outside (diagram 1), then diving under the other rider or riders as they exit on the outside. This is called a swooper pass. It can be surprisingly effective.

When you're in second place and close to the lead as you enter the turn, it may be to your benefit to enter the turn from a center-of-the track position, and also come out of the turn in the middle of the track (diagram 2).

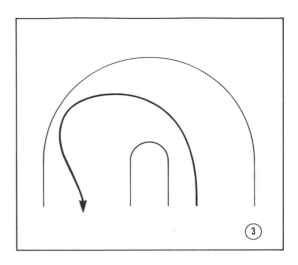

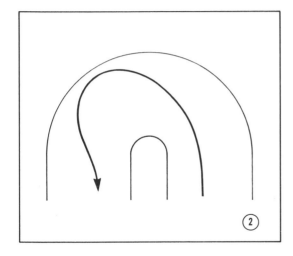

A more aggressive way to block a rider who is just behind you is to tighten the turn on the inside, perhaps forcing your opponent to brake hard, and

If you're leading the race, the best strategy is to go into the turn on the inside and exit on the outside (diagram 3). This prevents any rider who is close from diving under you and snatching the lead.

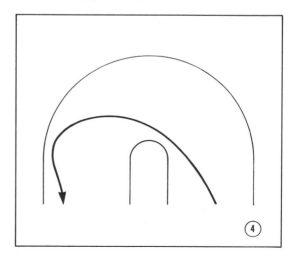

Reckless driving is a frequent cause of spills.

going wider to the outside as you exit (diagram 4).

No matter how you execute the turn, remember to keep your inside pedal up. Otherwise, it can dig into the ground as you bank—and send you sprawling.

If you're holding down the lead, you can pretty much ride your own race, deciding what line to take on turns and how fast to hit the bumps. But if you're trailing the field, you have to take chances.

This shouldn't imply that you should ever be reckless. Recklessness is the chief cause of accidents and injuries in BMX racing. It takes guts to be successful in BMX, but recklessness is overdoing it.

Cutting off an opponent is one common form of recklessness. Often it occurs when one rider rips past another and then swings in front of the passed rider. There's not sufficient clearance. The rear wheel of the bike in front brushes the front wheel of the trailing bike. Both riders go down.

Cutting off another biker doesn't make sense. A collision is frequently the result. And you can't win a race when you are on the ground. As a rule of thumb, be sure that you are at least a full bicycle length ahead of a rival before cutting in front.

Not only can reckless riding lead to an accident, it's also unwise from the standpoint of tactics. If you're found guilty of cutting off another rider or some other rash move, you could be disqualified for unsafe riding.

You can also be disqualified for lashing out and kicking or pushing an opponent during a race. Elbowing, which is not uncommon, can also be a reason for disqualification.

No matter how careful you are as a rider, there are times when you are going to hit the dirt. The chances are that you'll end up with nothing more than a bruise or scrape.

You can help prevent broken bones or other serious injuries by knowing how to fall. The trick is to try to land on one shoulder and tuck your chin to your chest. Bring your knees up and roll across your back.

What you don't want to do is hit the ground stiffly, landing on an outstretched arm or leg. Whenever possible, let your shoulders and upper body absorb the impact of the spill.

BIKE CARE

BMX bikes are stronger and better designed than any bikes in history. Their parts are the finest the industry has to offer. Still, your BMX bike has to be kept clean and properly tuned. Otherwise, it's not going to perform as it should.

Keep the bike clean so it will retain its slick, good looks. Never use a hose to clean it. Instead, wipe it clean with a damp rag, then apply a good quality polish.

Make a habit of inspecting the bike after every ride. Listen for squeaks, knocks, or scraping noises. Give the machine a careful visual inspection, too.

Here are some items to check:

HANDLEBARS—Test for looseness. If there is the slightest bit of wobble, tighten the head bolt atop the stem.

FRONT FORK—If there is any play in the front fork, loosen the locking nut at the top of the headset tube. Then tighten the adjusting cup to take up the play. Last, retighten the locknut.

TIRES—The correct tire pressure is embossed on the side of each tire. Check the pressure once a week with a reliable gauge. Riding with pressure at less than recommended levels can cause cuts or ruptures in the tire surfaces and pinch and tear inner tubes.

WHEELS—Turn the bike upside down so that it rests on the handlebars and seat. Spin the front

To check handlebars for looseness, straddle front wheel like this, then try turning the bars.

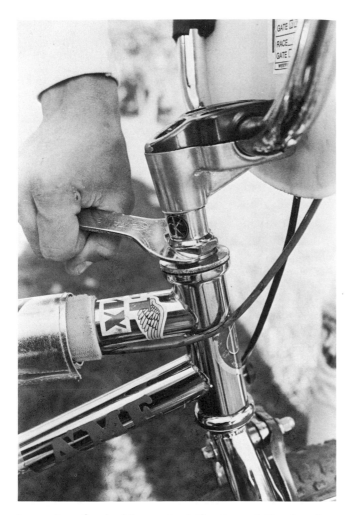

Loosening the locking nut at the top of the headset tube.

Keep the tires at the correct air pressure.

Inspecting the front wheel for wobble.

wheel and sight along it. You want to be sure there's no wobble and that it's centered properly between the forks.

If there is wobble, it may mean the rim is bent. Or perhaps the bearings are worn and require adjustment.

Check the spokes as the wheel turns by pulling at them one by one with your index finger, almost as if each is a guitar string. Each spoke should give off a *ping*. Those that emit a *thunk* need tightening. It shouldn't be necessary, however, to tighten any spoke more than ¼ or ½ of a turn.

Take hold of a pedal and crank it to spin the rear wheel, then inspect the wheel and its spokes.

CHAIN—Check the chain for tension. Put a couple of fingers under the chain at a point about midway between the front and rear sprockets, or press down on it from above with your thumb. You should not be able to move the chain up or down by more than half an inch. If you can move it any more than that, the chain is too loose, and it could jump off the sprocket as you pedal. If you can't move it more than a quarter of an inch, the chain is too tight. It can snap under heavy pressure.

To adjust chain tension, loosen the rear axle nuts and slide the wheel forward or back in the dropout slots. Tighten the axle nuts once the chain is adjusted.

Lubricate the chain with a few drops of light motor oil about once a month. When necessary,

Here's how to check the chain for the right amount of tension.

you release the brake, the pads should spring out from the rim. The narrower the clearance between the pads and the rim, the less time it will take you to apply the brakes.

PEDALS—Spin the pedals. If they don't spin fast, apply lubricant.

FRAME—After every race, or anytime you subject the bike to a hard ride, inspect the frame carefully. Be sure there are no bends or bows in the metal tubing.

Use a magnifying glass and look for hairline cracks within or adjacent to each welded joint. Even the tiniest crack means trouble. It can only get bigger and lead to a complete breakdown. Have the crack repaired before you use the bike again.

clean the chain with a brush dipped in paint thinner or solvent. Then relubricate it.

BRAKES—The slim control cable that is common to caliper brakes, the type of brakes used on BMX bikes, can stretch slightly under heavy use. If you are beginning to have problems stopping, you may need to increase the tension of the cable. It's easy to do. Loosen the bolt that holds the cable on the brake, squeeze the brake pads to the rim, then pull the cable a bit tauter, and retighten the bolt. When

Loosening the bolt that holds the brake cable.

This is only a partial list of the maintenance chores you should perform on a regular basis. What else you do depends on the knowledge and experience you have in bike repair. Don't try to solve serious problems unless you are completely sure of what you are doing. Instead, take the bike to a reputable repair shop.

Don't fail to give your bike the care it requires. In return, you'll get many hundreds of hours of enjoyable riding.

BMX ORGANIZATIONS

There are many different groups and organizations involved in BMX racing. These organizations make rules, issue racing licenses, and keep the point totals that determine local, national, and regional rankings.

The American Bicycle Association (ABA) and the National Bicycle League (NBL) are the most important BMX organizations. They sanction races at more than 700 tracks throughout the country. Other tracks are affiliated with local or regional sanctioning organizations.

Most race meets attract many hundreds of riders. A system of qualifying is necessary to reduce the number of contestants to the best eight riders in each class. These eight riders then compete in the final race, called the main (short for main event).

In the NBL, the moto system is used to determine the qualifiers. In the ABA, the transfer system is used.

Under the rules of the moto system, you compete in three motos, facing the same riders in each race. Points are awarded in each moto—1 point for

finishing first, 2 points for finishing second, 3 points for third, and so forth.

The riders with the lowest point totals for the three motos move into a semi-main (a semifinal race). Suppose rider A places second, first, and sixth in the three motos. That would give rider A nine points $(2 + 1 + 6 = 9)$. Rider B finishes first, fourth and third. Rider B would have a total of eight points $(1 + 4 + 3)$. He also would have earned the right to move into a semi-main ahead of rider A.

Under the terms of the ABA's transfer system, you also compete in three motos. But you must finish first in one of the motos in order to transfer to a semi-main. As soon as you're declared a winner in a moto, you don't have to race again until your semi.

Once you are entered in a semi, the NBL's moto system and the ABA's transfer system become much the same. The top four finishers in each semi transfer to the next set of semis or to the main. The finishing order in the main determines the champion.

No matter which organization sanctions the races at the track where you plan to compete, certain standard rules will apply. One important rule states that you will compete within your own age group. Sometimes there may not be enough entrants to fill the eight slots in the starting gate, so two age groups will be combined. But, generally, you'll compete against riders who are the same age as you are.

You must register before the race and pay an entry fee, usually from $3 to $5. This fee helps to pay the track operating expenses and goes toward the purchase of trophies. You must agree to wear the proper clothing, which includes a helmet and mouth protector, a wrist-length shirt, long pants, and so forth. You must permit your bike to be inspected before the race. You must be ready in your position at the starting gate when your moto is called.

For additional information concerning the rules of racing, write the principal sanctioning organizations. Here are their addresses:

American Bicycle Association
P.O. Box 718
Chandler, AZ 85224

National Bicycle League
84 Park Avenue
Flemington, NJ 08822

GLOSSARY

ABA—The American Bicycle Association, one of the organizations that governs BMX racing.

BARS—Short for handlebars.

BERM—A high-banked turn.

BMX—Abbreviation for bicycle motocross.

BOTTOM BRACKET—The short tube at the bottom of the bicycle frame into which the crank axle and crank bearings fit.

CALIPER BRAKES—Hand brakes; they are operated by handlebar-mounted levers.

CHAIN—The unit that transmits power from the chainwheel (or front sprocket) to the rear wheel.

CHAIN STAYS—The section of the bicycle frame from the bottom bracket to the rear wheel dropouts.

CHAINWHEEL—The large wheel with gear teeth on the right crank that delivers power from the pedal and crank, through the chain, to the rear wheel. Also called the front sprocket.

CHROME-MOLY—Short for chrome molybdenum.

COASTER BRAKE—A bicycle brake activated by back pressure on the pedals.

COG—The rear sprocket or freewheel.

CRANK—The metal rotating arm to which the pedal attaches.

CRUISER CLASS—A BMX racing class of adult riders who compete on 24- or 26-inch bikes.

DIRECT TRANSFER—*See* Transfer system

DOWN TUBE—The part of the bicycle frame that extends from the head tube to the bottom bracket.

DRIVE TRAIN—The system that powers the bicycle and includes the pedals, cranks, chain, front and rear sprockets, and rear wheel.

DROPOUT—A slot at the bottom of a fork and stay into which an axle fits.

ENDO—A trick in which the bike is stopped abruptly, causing it to tilt forward on the front wheel.

FREESTYLE—Trick riding.

FREEWHEEL—The rear sprocket; also called the cog.

FRONT FORK—The steering assembly that holds the front wheel.

FRONT SPROCKET—*See* Chainwheel

GEAR RATIO—A number that tells you how many times the rear wheel will revolve for every revolution of the pedals. The gear ratio is found by dividing the number of teeth in the chainwheel by the number of teeth in the rear sprocket.

GOOSENECK—*See* Handlebar stem

GUSSET—A metal brace added at a joint as reinforcement.

HANDLEBAR STEM—The clamp that holds the handlebars; the bottom part of the stem fits into the head tube. Also called the gooseneck or stem.

HEAD—*See* Head tube

HEADSET—The bearing assembly within the steering head.

HEAD TUBE—The large-diameter metal tube that holds the front fork and bearings. Also called the steering head.

HOLDING AREA—The area adjacent to a track where bicycles are stored before a race.

HOLESHOT—A tactic that enables you to jump into the lead at the race's start.

HUB—The units within the front and rear wheels which house the bearings and axles and hold the spoke ends.

KICKTURN—A trick involving a ramp in which you ride the bike to near the top, pivot it around 180 degrees on its rear wheel, then lower the front wheel and pedal down the ramp.

KNOBBY—A bicycle tire with large knobs on the tread for traction.

LEATHERS—The pants of the BMX uniform.

MAG WHEELS—Spokeless wheels reinforced with heavy struts.

MAIN—The final race in a class; the main event.

MEET—The entire program of races.

MOTO—A single race or preliminary heat.

MOTOCROSS—A motorcycle race over rugged terrain. The term comes from "motorcycle" and "cross-country."

MOTO SHEET—The official listing of riders, the motos in which they will compete, plus their gate positions for each moto.

MOTO SYSTEM—A method of scoring common to NBL events in which each rider competes in three motos. The riders with the best finishes or the most points earned for those finishes advance to the semi-main.

NBL—The National Bicycle League, one of the organizations that governs BMX racing.

OFF-CAMBER—A turn that is banked slightly to the outside.

PIT AREA—The area of a track near the starting line where last-minute adjustments are made.

RAD, RADICAL—Anything that is exceptional in nature.

RIM—The outer circle of the bicycle wheel.

SADDLE—The bicycle seat.

SAFETY PADS—Cushioning material that covers the handlebar crossbar, the top tube, and the stem.

SANCTION—The authorization for holding a race meet according to established rules and regulations.

SANCTIONED RACE—Race conducted under an association's rules and regulations.

SEAT POST—The metal rod that holds the seat; the bottom end of the seat post fits into the seat tube.

SEAT STAYS—The parts of the bicycle frame that extend from beneath the seat to the rear wheel axle and dropouts.

SEAT TUBE—The metal tube into which the seat post fits; it extends from beneath the seat to the bottom bracket.

SEMI-MAIN—The next-to-last race of a meet.

SPROCKET—A toothed, chain-driven wheel.

STEERING HEAD—*See* Head tube

STEM—*See* Handlebar stem

SWOOPER—A type of pass in which you enter a turn on the outside and exit on the inside with the idea of passing—swooping by—opposing riders.

TABLETOP—A flat-topped jump.

TAKE AIR—To hurtle the bike into the air so that both wheels come off the ground.

TOP TUBE—The horizontal metal tube that extends from the steering head to the seat tube.

TRANSFER—To place high enough in one race to be able to advance to the next level of competition.

TRANSFER SYSTEM—A system of scoring common to ABA meets in which any rider finishing first in a moto is advanced to the semi-main; also called direct transfer.

WHEELIE—A trick in which you ride with the front wheel off the ground.

WHOOP—A bump.

WHOOP-DE-DOOS—A series of bumps in a track; also called whoops.

WIPEOUT—A spill or fall.